MW00954840

This book belongs to:

____

Made in the USA
Columbia, SC
08 January 2022

53900073R20061